Meridian

Meridian

Nancy Gaffield

Longbarrow Press

Published in 2019 by
Longbarrow Press
76 Holme Lane
Sheffield
S6 4JW

www.longbarrowpress.com

Printed by T.J. International Ltd,
Padstow, Cornwall

All rights reserved

Poems © Nancy Gaffield 2019
Photographs © Nancy Gaffield 2019
Jacket design © Brian Lewis 2019

ISBN 978-1-906175-37-5

First edition

Contents

11   I: Peacehaven to Greenwich

35   II: Greenwich to Hardwick

61   III: Hardwick to Boston

83   IV: Boston to Sand le Mere

108   *Bibliography*

109   *Acknowledgements*

I take SPACE to be the central fact
to [wo]man born in America.
Charles Olson, *Call Me Ishmael*
[Nancy Gaffield]

There is nothing stronger than a woman
who has rebuilt herself.
Hannah Gadsby, *Nanette*

> The key difference between a trail and a path is directional: paths extend forward, whereas trails extend backward.
> Robert Moor, *On Trails: An Exploration*

The idea was to walk the line from Peacehaven to the Humber. I had devised the notion that the physical act of walking would help me to locate what was lost. It started with Jeremy's singing: "How shall we remember them?" It led to this. All I had to do was follow the Meridian Line on the Ordnance Survey maps—heading always north. True north.

Armed with an iPhone, its camera, a recording app, the route would bear me from sea to shining sea along a temporal divide. Defying time. Defying space.

Travelling light—a stick for steep terrain, a compass for the forest, waterproofs for the rain, a rucksack—I would walk alone, though never averse to the kindness of strangers or the company of a good dog.

This is a walking practice.

I

Peacehaven
to Greenwich

ORDNANCE SURVEY MAP 122: BRIGHTON & HOVE

Peacehaven to Lewes

And then I see the views out
    to the sea in the south
        & across the Weald
  in the north
      a high chalk ridge
  under a glassine sky

                a space of enunciation

trace landscapes
    vacant lots
        a pivotal place

the fields lie fallow
    waiting for rain
        waiting for the yoke

walking in / walking out
    looking for the gap
        in the hedge

the hole
    in the tree
        an aperture

in the season of absolute light
    before harvest
        prefaces the closing down

Listen for the undersong
    sounds I cannot
        name / locate

            Disturbances within the threshold
            of hearing are sampled in time.
            The song that the rigging makes,
            Port of Gloucester. The acoustics
            of the sea. Here / there

the wind is constant
    the roll call of the dead
        is etched on my heart

    Every day the list increases.

            Meridian: The great circle of the
            celestial sphere that passes through
            its poles and the observer's zenith.
            The imposition of a mental map
            upon physical topography.

We arrive at Peacehaven
    municipal modernism
    clinging to principles

    the trai[ia]l begins
amongst terraced houses of marine
stucco   severed
coast land gives way
    to farmland

Reliable markers include long
barrows cairns dolmens ponds
springs wells castles churches
hill-forts quarries notches-in-hills
crossroads

This is a spatial practice.

In an argument with vertigo I make my way along the cliff-top
    clutching a fence wire
        posted: No Nude Bathing

below the tide
    shudders
        the shingle

above the grains of the north
    oats rye barley
        & a few sheep

At last I come upon the George V monument
    disappointing
        derelict land Charles Neville chose

naming it
    New-Anzac-on-Sea
        but after Gallipoli

he changed it
    to Peacehaven

    its most striking feature is a tablet
        listing the azimuths
            of the cities of empire

                c.1936 an empire
                standing on the landing

        Things correspond.

The hottest of summer suns
quickens the heart

high streets of bookmakers
take-aways charity shops

a passing bus
sends up whirlwinds of dust

      turning inland now
      across overgrown parkland
      whistling a happy tune

          —He led her home
          Through the barley fields
          Where the saffron poppies grew.

      Dear Helen, is that you?

her voice swirls
—a bit like Crab Nebula

Abandoned backwaters   waste lots
    yield to row houses
        low bungalows

    The man in the street says: "I've
    lived here all my life. I'm telling
    you there's no road in or out. You
    could slip into a ditch. No one
    would ever find you."

  The view composes.

I cup a hand to an ear to listen
   for her voice

hearing only the shingle's thunder
   or a storm edging in
     from the south

     —you have been in my mind
     between my toes
     agate

climbing the limestone cliffs
   following the South Downs Way
     the scent of geraniums
   infuses the day

path overcome by nettles then brambles
   the cartwheel flower
     (impassable)

to Telescombe Tye
   open field
     commons

a small cluster of sheep
    lowing
        avoid eye contact
  (we do)

no debt crisis here
    no detonation or detention
        nor white noise

only this church
    dedicated to St Lawrence
        patron saint of archives

"We want it for all time"
    so it remains
        at the dead end of a winding

no one stirs in this place that time forgot
    how many pairs of eyes are watching
        from behind net curtains?

in a graveyard
    thoughts unfold
        how to live
    without a daughter
        at the end
    what to do

            —mourn the loss
            of people
            no wild bird does

No one walks the path today
        nor am I clear
                where it goes
        when it disappears
                into shadows

a scattering of farm buildings
        screened by police cars
                twisted remnants of fence

rusted machinery
        Friesian cattle in stalls
                sound of chewing

on the wall of the barn
        a plaque marks
                the Greenwich Meridian

six officers armed with assault rifles
        Lorne Malvo ruthless contract killer drawls
        —There are no saints in the animal kingdom.
        Only breakfast and dinner.

Walking away
from this pantomime
[un]evenly following the road
        I don't know how
I came to be here
only all those years ago
I knew I would be
thinking back to that moment
when I saw myself here

the sound of the wind
        murmuring
                the birch

Lewes to East Grinstead

—They would, she thought, going on again, however long they lived, come back to this night…
  Virginia Woolf, *To the Lighthouse*

we are all connected
        all experiences
                are along a continuum

What is a line
a length
without breadth
      the trace of
            a moving point
      a procedure

                        light
                        framed in astragals

everyone wants to
die at home
      I'm inside
            that train whistle
      sickness for / of

I don't know how
to go there

                  —in the fragrant pines
              and the cedars dusk and dim

I only know walking
is involved in it.

The geese pass in high skeins
    autumn is coming

I am six years old again
    learning to read
        the landscape

making my way by sight by history
    by the compass
        by luck

imagining the lines of longitude
    as twin ropes
        of a swing

in the left hand is Sussex
    in the right the 105th Meridian West
        UTC-7:00 Mountain Time North

the Prospect Road interchange
    in Fort Collins aligns
        almost precisely along it

it also passes through
    Union Station
        in Denver

    —*I wander thro' each charter'd street*
      mountain towns
        (Stout, COLO Pop. 47 ½)

Don't look back
>or you will plunge
>>into terrae incognitae

night terrors
>devoid
>>of any coordinates

the haggard dawn pulls
>you from your bed
>>it's time to go
>a-wanderin

>>>The face on the barroom floor in actual fact belonged to Edna "Nita" Davis, 1936. Gold made Central City, a red-dirt town, the richest square mile on earth. Here was the lure of the foreign back in your own back yard.

I cut myself free
>adrift now
>>in the outer limits

>This is a tale of two continents.

An observant solitary woman
        strolls the South Downs Way
she is no armchair traveller
        but a non-paying customer
in a commercial world
        walking along at crab pace
sometimes sideways
        crossing the pond
she steps into the water
        her pockets brimming
            with the eyes of the dead

        How far we have come to go home again.

Coming into woods now
        following scent trails
            vapour trails

counting steps & channelling
        Grandma Hazard
            our simian arms

swinging at the elbow
        that final flick
            of the wrist

I walk with empty hands
        amongst the nut-gatherers
            tracking an impression

after those that made it
        have passed by
            presence in absence

I walk through dappled wood
    where the nut-gatherers
        course

yellow leaf-fall
    snake casings
        parasols and other fungi

knots fold into gnarls
    lines of genealogy
        kinship

twilight flickers through
    gaps in the trees
        a path of light

ORDNANCE SURVEY MAP 135:
ASHDOWN FOREST

Not a forest of wooded trees
    but a tangle of bracken & gorse
medieval rabbit warrens
    abandoned sandstone quarries

skylarks in song-flight above
    streams stained red with iron &
"the insatiable desire of pasture
    for sheep and cattel"

    (Landscape remembers.)

Danehill [Anglo-Saxon for swine pasture on the hill]
    is surrounded by woods
        Cowstock Wood
        Down Wood
        Enholm's Wood
        High Wood
        Withy Wood
        Sedge Wood
            "thick and inaccessible"
                (the Venerable Bede)

iteration a form of salvage

enclosed with a fence & a ditch
    they named The Pale
        you dare not go beyond it

lost genera:
    bear
    wolf
    wildcat

playground for Henry (he hunted
    Anne)

iron lodging in the haematite
    rust-red streaks
        hard but brittle

scrub forest
    the haunt of the jackdaw
      kiaw   *kiaw*
        O come back

Knotted bank of weed and wildflower
    opens out to arable fields
split by hedgerows of hawthorn
    & dog rose thick with hips

a dying world lying under the wing
    of London

I am a migrant too

am a stranger in this land
    am no stranger
        to its undoing

Tessellation of gravestones
    squirrels decipher
        a detour

through the pyracantha
        resplendent in orange
                but poisonous

     O wild seed in Aftonland

pistillate
     bract
          bole
               taper
                    axis
                        I lie down
                    on bare ground
               shadow-tackled in
          leaf-whelm
     as the stump
gives way

What is a line?
    A long thin mark
    A queue of people
    A remark intended to entertain or persuade
    The route followed by a railroad track
    A row of positions to defend against attack
    Forked lightning
    A unit of language in a poem
    A short sequence of musical notes
    A sometimes imaginary mark that forms an edge
    or a border
    An umbilical cord

            —And what of the Line? Of imperial
            dreams and dead men, all that
            remained was long grass.

                ::

Northern monochrome
    this is the place
        of consolation

fragrant black cedar
    dripping with rain
        the estuary invisible
    but for the tang of the oyster farms

                In Tillamook Helen sang her ballads
                to a room of fisherfolk. In the
                window behind them she traced
                the network of lines connecting
                the boats as one by one their lamps
                were lit. She invoked the wind to
                take what remained of her to the
                four corners of the room &
                further still across the sea to the
                northern churchyard with its
                gravestones stacked against each
                other, on top the death card
                reversed [unable to move on].

    This is a game for lichen for crows
    —*I am the self-consumer of my woes.*

In the woods where the words live
    I huddle down between square brackets
        the making of a woman is not silence
or violence
    but her freedom to roam
        in woods / words

Let go of surmise & begin again.

ORDNANCE SURVEY MAP 162: GREENWICH & GRAVESEND

Oxted to Greenwich

This part of town isn't meant
    to be gawked at
newly-built business parks
    abut abandoned warehouses
brownfield sites
    ripe for development
in the distance the yelp of a dog

> "It was said that the Powder of Sympathy could help sailors to find longitude. Every ship was to carry a live dog that had been scratched by the same knife, kept in London. At Noon each day, the knife would be plunged into the Powder of Sympathy, causing the dog to yelp with pain. The ship's captain would then know it was exactly Noon in London. It proved totally useless."
>   National Maritime Museum

This is the house that Wren built
    it was never ours   the picket fence
the good dog [here boy]
    the bone

::

                Circumpolar stars—clock stars—
                never rise nor set. These were used to
                align the telescope known as the Airy
                Transit Circle.

The relationship between telescope
        & clock
                is collateral

an astronomer observes
        the transit of a celestial body
                he marks it by the clock
        & the clock takes stock

zero degrees
        begins at the Airy Transit Circle telescope
                housed in the Meridian Building

today a large group of Chinese tourists
        pose with one foot in the east
                another in the west

At Greenwich Astronomia holds
        the moon in her right hand
        & the sun in her left
        but no woman has ever held
        the post of Astronomer Royal

Who will remember Tompion's 14-foot pendulum clocks
        accurate enough for Flamsteed
        to conclude the constancy
        of the earth's movement?

Who will remember Shortt's free-pendulum clock
        showing that the speed of earth's rotation
        is not so constant after all?

Who will remember the Star Room
        with its walnut-panelled octagonal walls
        where we stood gazing at an ever expanding universe
        its ordinary matter of planets & stars
        toward a future we could never hope for

—*Stars swarmed. Headlands washed in the seas.*

And if I'm not at sea
        what is this
        turbulence

you said it always takes the same amount of time
for the pendulum to swing:

$$T = 2\pi \sqrt{\left(\frac{l}{g}\right)}$$

        [T = 2 pi root "l" over "g" where "l"
        is pendulum length and "g" is
        gravitational acceleration]

harmonic motion   though there are drawbacks
        we won't go into here

and if it fails
        when the rocking starts
how is one to locate
        home-time

it is the penultimate day
        of your life

and if I commend you
        to the deep
my Gloucester man
        what use the star atlas
the hemisphaerium

Notes to Part I

Throughout *Meridian*, I use the dash [—] for quoted lines. Italicized lines can also be quotes, but are always overheard speech or language spoken aloud; where quotation marks appear, they are either direct discourse or a quotation from a text.

Part I is introduced by Robert Moor's notion that paths are forward-going whereas trails are backward-looking. In this poem, I am following the Greenwich Meridian Trail as a path, walking forward in a northerly direction. Insofar as I am recalling snippets from books, scenes from films, or events, I am following a trail backwards.

p.13. "The act of walking is to the urban system what the speech act is to language or to the statements uttered. At the most elementary level, it has a triple 'enunciative' function: it is a process of *appropriation* of the topographical system on the part of the pedestrian; it is a spatial acting-out of the place; and it implies relations among differentiated positions, that is, among pragmatic 'contracts' in the form of movements. It thus seems possible to give a preliminary definition to walking as a space of enunciation." Michel de Certeau, *The Practice of Everyday Life*.

p.16. Helen Adam's ghost appears with the saffron poppies; the phrase "swirling like Crab Nebula" is from a letter Charles Olson wrote to Helen Feinstein. I met Helen in 1979 when she came to read in Newport, Oregon. Helen wanted to look for agates in Newport's many rock shops; we spent a pleasant day together scavenging through boxes, looking for the rarest and most expensive: the water agate. The water trapped inside them is over one hundred million years old.

p.18. Lorine Niedecker's poem 'North Central'.

p.19. Walking in an unfamiliar landscape, you encounter the unexpected. It's alarming to see a remote farm surrounded by police cars with armed men. It turns out to be a film crew. I think of Billy Bob Thornton in *Fargo*. His character's name is Lorne Malvo.

p.20. A line from Whitman's powerful elegy, 'When Lilacs Last in the Dooryard Bloom'd'.

p.21. In Blake's poem the "charter'd streets" refers to the system of commercial management that existed in his day. That same system appears in nature, too. Blake is saying that even the River Thames is managed for profit; the same can be said of the countryside.

p.25. The Venerable Bede (672-735) was an English monk and Anglo-Saxon scholar who wrote on a number of subjects, including nature, the Bible, history, music and poetry. His most famous work is *The Ecclesiastical History of the English People*. He described the land between the North and South Downs, known as Anderida's Wood and later The Weald, as "thick and inaccessible".

p.27. Richard Flanagan writes of the Burma Railway in *The Narrow Road to the Deep North*; railways are another kind of line.

p.28. The poet John Clare is a constant companion. "I am the self-consumer of my woes" is from his poem 'I Am'.

p.31. Boris Pasternak's 'The Racing Stars'. This poem is an elegy to a close friend who died at the time of writing. He was introduced to me in Olson's Gloucester (Massachusetts).

II

Greenwich
to Hardwick

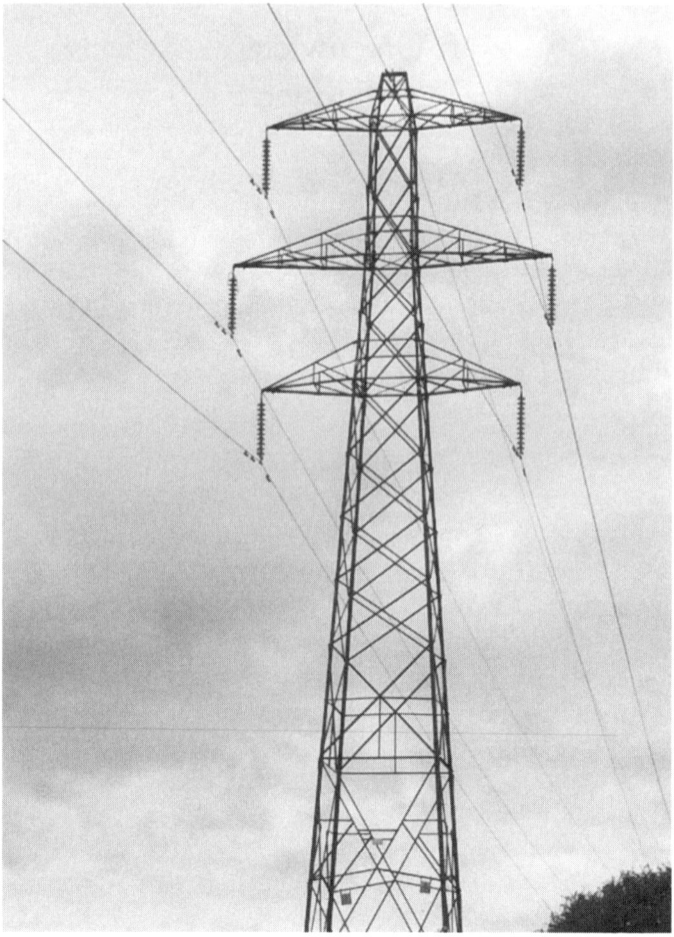

ORDNANCE SURVEY MAP 162: GREENWICH & GRAVESEND

—Before it's too late. She will. Get it down. Herself. The truth.

        Iain Sinclair, *Lights Out for the Territory*

Greenwich to Stratford

An occasion
Greenwich railway station to St Alfege
                (Hawksmoor's design)
    turned back to front
the spot where Alfege
        frail   uncertain   afraid
was killed
a thousand years ago
        but resolved
    his bailout would cut too deep

to Church Lane to
ship's mast
in thick fog
    Ghost Sark
        tramping for cargoes in Eastern seas
                still waters rust deep

derelict sites
an independent author
uncomfortable in the warmth of
    pukka jeans

unpredictable   industrial
proposed walk   cranes
    forced to adapt
    underground
    underwater

the tunnel 50 feet deep / 370 metres long
flickering interference of upper shield
second-hand light   ALERTS
    heading for
the Isle of Dogs
bow of the Thames

signature trace products
read like tide marks

    Brown & Lennox chain-cables
    McDougalls Self-Raising Flour
    Maconochie's Pan Yan Pickle
        "The Unlucky Isle of Dogs"

playful collages & compounded words
fit so neatly alongside
the meditation of the trail
a ductus
the details of the scheme
Greenwich to Chingford

to say nothing of the river
    where a gulp of cormorants
        line the dock
            not to be confused with a shag

Leave the Thames Path & follow
the signs to Narrow Street

    The Grapes was on the river then
        they say the watermen
        led drunken patrons
        to the river & later
        sold their bodies for dissection

inside the Cosy
delectable drinks
    Purl   Flip   Dog's Nose

        "…when the light shone full upon the grain of certain panels, and particularly upon an old corner cupboard of walnut-wood in the bar, you might trace little forests there."

being faint-hearted I stand outside
looking at the linens drying on the line

        ::

Watery boundary
    with its tongue lolling
alluvial land
    home to residential Poplar (no trees)

first settlement appears in the 12th century
    80 acres of arable & a windmill

an early map c.1740 identifies
    Limehouse Hole
    The Breach
    Great Gut
    Killing Ground

constant flooding leads to abandonment
    reclamation
    quagmired in separateness

a noticeably windy place so in the 18th century
    windmills   wharves   shipbreakers
    the iron trade

geomancers fancied the flattening fields

cynocephalic outlaw land
    scavenging from the kills
        larger predators make

north of the ragged tunnel
    north-minded
        I can't walk through

reroute through a housing estate
    turn right through metal gates
    shunt through the park
    to the towpath

Limehouse the target
sponsor of The Cut
    far too neat
        "decidedly picturesque" (Pevsner)

from here you could travel by canal boat
nearly all the way to Kendal

ORDNANCE SURVEY MAP 174: EPPING FOREST & LEA VALLEY

—Who you walk with alters what you see.
          Iain Sinclair, *Lights Out for the Territory*

Stratford to Chingford

I walk with Kat Peddie
she sets the pace out of Leytonstone
brisk
we walk up Cann Hall Road
under the railway
follow the path to Jubilee Pond
enter Epping Forest
Waltham Abbey our goal

Speaking of Virgil

          —On their way to Italy
          the Trojans make a detour to hell

we summon the Low-ghost
consult the compass
watch where the paths divide
follow the needlepoint
          North

Kat stops to photograph the twin towers
overlooking Wanstead flats
there's talk of demolition

in-between-ness *nepantia*
             unstable
                  fragile
                            perilous
                       fleeting
                  evanescent

      Like Daedalus   fleeing the realm
we have landed here in ancient woodland
with a giant ball of string
an infamous place
of unsolved crime   lost
keepsakes   part
of the tableau
enjoying pre-ballot optimism
two days before the assembled
crowd X us out

we scout the wood's white-topped posts
to Leyton Flats & Hollow Pond
shrinking under a hot sun
to a deep depression
thick with brambles
where Whipps Cross Lido
used to be
                  precarios

if language is
migrant
if our bodies are
migrant

where does that leave us
except
at the forest's fringe
on the summer solstice
Kat's wearing shorts
& we're still in the union

>*—I'm going into the woods on a path I have no idea about. I'm not going to look backwards on the path at all or make Indian signs on the trees to see where I am.*

we talk of what the outside means
in poetry   in language
lineal women
        civilly
              disobedient

we make a space of appearance
acting & speaking together
sharing words and deeds

      —anywhere people gather
          is polis

registering the thunder's peal
ourself alone

we pause to photograph a tree
      struck by lightning
           though the centre's charred
      the canopy flourishes

This is the place where dog lines circle
back on themselves amongst crack willow

    Waltham Abbey was too far.

Chingford to Waltham Abbey

This time walking untethered
    in this site of transition
        the trail branches & twines

I weave my way through
    ferns the height of me
        in the forest's chlorophyllic glow

the lines of longitude and latitude a seine
    to drag the sea for fish
        & memories

        precarios

"Discovering the longitude" was a term for
attempting the impossible
the butt of jokes   like pigs flying
until Harrison's H1 clock
changed everything

The poet should be like the scientist
"who begins by learning
what has been discovered already"

    Einstein's beautiful theory
    only a hundred years old
    overthrew Euclidian space / Newtonian gravity

an infinite number of times may co-exist
here / there
past / present
are relative & change
according to the ordinates and coordinates
you select

   —I have had to learn the simplest things last

Charles Mason & Jeremiah Dixon
Harrison's contemporaries went down to the sea
in ships to the Cape of Good Hope
to map the transit of Venus
in a chain of Cause
and Effect that line would ~~resolve~~
result in a border dispute
  time is longitude
  longitude time
    whistling Dixie

    ::

Pole Hill straddles the border
between Greater London & Essex
London 10.96 miles in the visible
  distance

the obelisk (1824) marks
the Meridian but
  in actual fact
    it passes 19 feet east of here
  on T.E. Lawrence's ground

Walking confirms the wood is the place
to begin to occupy the poetics of space
   by poetics I mean poetry
      which comes whilst walking
     amongst ferns Clare would recognise
      heading the same way
    towards Lincolnshire

I am wary of the stranger
   on the path
     without a dog
naming as I walk
   picking things out
     oak beech hornbeam
       recognising the smooth
  fluted bark
      the males adorned in drooping catkins

beware the aether
& who controls it

        now we enter
        a hostile environment
        shapes in the shadows
        dark forces are at work
        when people feel they are
        given permission

I stoop to remove
   a snail clinging to my ankle
     following Clare
up the Great North Road
   amongst ancient pollarded trees
    recording
      the boundary

walking the route
    noting the landmarks
        rivers / roads / trees / stones
    naming as I walk

Every forest collects its ghosts
enfolds them into lyric
history   I watch the path
lose ground   the path
double-crosses

> *—Doubt and hopelessness made me turn so feeble that I was scarcely able to walk*

Petrichor of asphalt
I emerge on the road
to Sewardstone
foot-foundered I hitch a ride
with a stranger
delivering parish magazines
the elusive Abbey
for another day

Waltham Abbey and its Garden, Epistle

Erin,
On the ceiling of the Abbey is an old man with an open book & a young man whose book is closed & sealed. Surrounding these are the four elements. They are the same & not the same. The signs of the zodiac are there. I am the gardener in the moon weeding the evil from the world. You are an old man half-animal half-fish sitting by the fire waiting for the resurrection. Christ the redeemer is a moth circling the flame. The repetition is its own resolution.

> *Christ above me*
> *Christ on my right*
> *Christ when I lie down*
> *Christ when I arise*

Leaving the medieval world I walk on through the gatehouse alongside Cornmill Stream & the dragonfly sanctuary remembering your father before he was a dragonfly, refusing to reveal what I am / not missing & here is proof of fortunate happenstance. I meet Graham and Hilda posting way-markers. We walk together a mile or two; they show me a large granite sculpture from the Old London Bridge.

> *London Bridge has fallen down & moved to Arizona*

This one sits behind a conifer tree. Its partner another kilometre north, both on the Meridian line.

I will find you
      maybe in a walled garden
      maybe in an orchard
      maybe on a towpath
      maybe in the mist over a weir
the clouds threaten rain   I take a photo
      to remember the day

ORDNANCE SURVEY MAP 194: HERTFORD & BISHOP'S STORTFORD

—Old is the body I wear
But I walk in the wind
As I run to the North
        Helen Adam, 'A Walk in the Wind'

Waltham Abbey to Royston

Late summer day on the autumn equinox
Wareside →Braughing
    (*come prepared / avoid backtracking*)
then doubling back to the Red Lion
once a monastery now a pub to begin again

The waitress is kind enough
but the man in the corner asks
too many questions
    should I or shouldn't I
talk to strangers   they may be better company
but will they ambush you afterwards
in a remote corner of the county?

    This is a lone place
where a long trail of sheep
tat the darkening sky

that woman in stone
keeps pace with me
    though I walk alone
following the track
observing the trees

> "At Round Wood you will cross
> The Greenwich Meridian
> stop to look south & catch a glimpse
> of Canary Wharf some 40 miles away
> your last view of London."

I do
the blue lines of One Canada Square
dissolve as I drop down the hill
to the valley & its bridge
over the River Rib at Barwick Ford

The line is a lodestar
& Hertfordshire a study in green and blue
a big sky watching each stalk
of corn   *a liminal place*
wide-open
spaces   where the wind
makes do   a desolate land
devoid of any single human
figure
only late September
squash blossoms in thrall
to the bevelled sun

> *—Unlike a drawn line*
> *a walked line can never be erased*

The day wears on
I walk against the clock

In
Gain
Again
Again[st]
    Against (*prep.*)

    (1) expressing motion towards: With hostile intent. Major General William Tecumseh Sherman marched against Meridian, Mississippi, on Valentine's Day 1864. http://americancivilwar.com/statepic/ms/ms012.html [Three months later, John Clare would be dead.]

    (2) expressing motion or action in opposition to someone or something: He ordered his men to wipe the place off the map. They did. The Confederate soldiers gainsaid it. Gainsay: to contradict, repudiate, fly in the face of. Shoot full of holes. They rebuilt the railways in 26 days.

    (3) expressing mutual opposition or relation: Hostile & active verbal & physical attitude, feeling & intention. In South Carolina three wounded at school, man dead at home. In California police shoot dead Ugandan refugee who pointed an e-cigarette against them. Again & again. ~~Orlando~~ Las Vegas worst mass shooting in modern US history. Again.

    (4) expressing position: The victim lies in the stairwell. Leans against the breezeblock, aggregate of ash bonded with cement. Winces at hard edges. Cracks & tears. Gaping. Can't stop it. Can't stop the flow.

    (5) expressing contact with pressure on or contiguity with someone or something: Overlapping views. Denial, dismissal, contrarian. Carbon passes the line of 400 parts per million. An ominous sign. Denial machine works overtime. Aggregate of industry, government, the fossil fuels lobby. Against reason.

    (6) in relation to time (*lit., obs.*): I walk north against the clock. Further & further north against the wind.

Perhaps I have taken things
too far   the poem
as spatial practice
writing along an invisible
line whose end is infinite
in this piece
of little England

the poem has become
a mayday call
an emergency
procedure   a distress signal
always given three times
in sequence:

MAYDAY MAYDAY MAYDAY
                        from French *venez m'aider*
                        meaning "come and help me"

            Newton's Third Law
    : force always comes in pairs
    a push or a pull
    that acts upon an object
    as a result of interactions

Late capitalism   has so much to answer for
we've used up   all the resources
                you can either
                      shut up
                      carry on as before
                      or adapt & survive

        I choose to walk
beginning again at Braughing
                sounds like *laughing*

comfortable weather
but for the sudden
sharp shower which comes
inevitably
long & often
    mother used to say
    you're neither sugar nor salt & you won't melt

I thought it strange & Swedish
   but it turned out
   to be Jonathan Swift

What does it mean
to go home
    disunited states

when a country elects a president
who says "*you can do anything*"
when you're a powerful man
"*they just let you do it*"
   "*fuck 'em*"
it's not just despicable
it's personal

   We drove by the old place
   no longer in the country Boulder
   spills across the plains all the way to Denver
   you say—*Look how they've let it go*
   I answer—*But that was half a century ago*
   so many things we remember
   differently

      like him standing at the back door
      lifting the butt of the shotgun to his shoulder
      drawing a bead on a figure zigzagging east
      across the fields
      to Marian's farm & safety

              he shucked them
              till all his desires
              slipped down
              their throat

    But today I'm at Braughing
it's the 7th of October
five days too late
for Old Man's Day
I hear him knocking
on the coffin wall
& no one is laughing

                ::

    At Ermine Street John
Clare & I part ways
his quest taking him further west
through St Neots
to Stilton   then Peterborough
      to Glinton
           & his Dulcinea
     Mary Joyce

In this play I am Don Quixote
tilting at windmills in the empty fields
of Hertfordshire

And I walk
And I walk   watching the country divide along a ghost line
And I walk
And I walk   remembering those high country fields
And I walk
And I walk   to the 12th century church at Little Hormead
And I walk
And I walk   trying to read the names on the tilting tombstones
And I walk
And I walk   wrapping up against the blue northers
And I walk
And I walk   breathing so deep I break

ORDNANCE SURVEY MAP 209: CAMBRIDGE

Royston to Hardwick

For the waters are come unto my soul

The signs of the zodiac shift. Earth orients towards Polaris. We begin afresh in the sign of Ophiculus, interpreter of dreams, seeker of peace & harmony, serpent-bearer haunting the archaic tracks of the northern sky. Where Ermine Street intersects with Icknield Way, ley-lines follow the chalk escarpment across the width of the land, one of four roads the Iceni named. A line that situates on St. Michael's Mount,

O let me not sink

Glastonbury Tor, Stonehenge, Avebury. We descend the long tunnel, for centuries filled with earth & rubbish & covered with a millstone. Darkness seeps across the floor.

I sink in deep mire where the floods overflow me

The dome complicated & numinous, the ceiling a beehive. Soft chalk aging unusually fast. Vibration & periodic cleaving away. Worms & small gnat larvae devour it. Millions of them. Leaks & worm casts bloat & erode the surface. The walls pour out hands & hearts open, energetic. Powerful healing man with a serpent. Seeker of enlightenment. Ten-pin bowling

I am weary of my crying

man with a skull in his right hand & a candle in his left.

For I am in trouble

Cooler & darker here at the bottom the carvings increase. St. Christopher patron saint of travellers holds an uprooted tree. A shrouded figure, a seated figure. St. Catherine with her spiked wheel. It flew apart into fragments. Calvary scene. Open hands & hearts double swirl & trouble. St. Lawrence with the grail of agate. His death in flames & fortitude. Three figures then a horse, an earth goddess & a shield. King David with arms uplifted.

For I am full of heaviness

One half of the millstone lies on the floor. Further square panels inserted over previous ones. A figure called Grave. At the western end, a crescent moon. Above a chimney for ventilation. Numerous niches & graffiti shoulder the centuries. Dampness gathers at our feet.

Hear me for I am poor & sorrowful

There is no way of knowing, no organic evidence or historical record. There was a skull. A skull was found in it.

Notes to Part II

Part II opens with a quotation from Iain Sinclair's *Lights Out for the Territory*. The first poem in this section is a cut-up. Individual words were plucked from the first ten pages and incorporated into it. In a similar way to Sinclair's tracing of routes through London, *Meridian* aims to follow the Prime Meridian along a section of Eastern England. The route travelled is more rural than urban, and by walking this route, I am interrogating the conflation of psychogeography and the flâneur, commonly a male wanderer of the urban environment.

p.38. "The Unlucky Isle of Dogs" is a quotation from Samuel Pepys' *Diaries*. The pub named The Grapes existed in Charles Dickens' time. Its description here is in *Our Mutual Friend*.

p.41. The Low-ghost refers to an idea elaborated by the American poet, Jack Spicer, in *The Collected Lectures*. It plays on 'Logos' or 'word'. In *The Collected Lectures*, Spicer elaborates his ideas about the serial poem. The poem (and the walk) was inspired by Spicer's notion that the poet does not drive the poem, but the poem drives the poet. However, this poem rejects Spicer's assertion that the serial poem moves forward without looking back.

p.43. The concept of polis is evoked here and throughout *Meridian*. Citing Hannah Arendt, I conceive of polis as that space where organized remembrance takes place. I take poetry to be such a place.

p.45. Ezra Pound in 'A Retrospect' advises the poet to begin by learning what has been discovered already.
    The reference to "seine" comes from Mark Twain's *Life on the Mississippi*: "When I'm playful I use the meridians of longitude and the parallels of latitude as a seine, and drag the Atlantic Ocean for whales."

p.46. "I have had to learn the simplest things last" is a line from Charles Olson's poem 'Maximus: to Himself'.

p.48. John Clare was a man displaced, a man walking through. He was in High Beach asylum for the mentally ill (Epping Forest) between 1837-41 when he met a group of travellers and walked away from there. The "doubt and hopelessness" is his line.

p.51. Hamish Fulton is a walking artist. Born in 1946, Fulton has made walking an art form, and since 1972, all his art is based on his experiences of walking.

p.55. In the 16th Century, there was a man who lived in Braughing who was believed to be dead. As the bearers were carrying his coffin to the funeral, they slipped and dropped the coffin, which "awoke" the sleeping man. He lived another 20 years but requested in his will that the date October 2 be an anniversary commemorating his "non-burial".

p.57-58. The italicised lines here are from Psalm 69. Royston Cave is at the intersection of Icknield Way and Ermine Street at Royston in Essex. See www.roystoncave.co.uk.

III

Hardwick to Boston

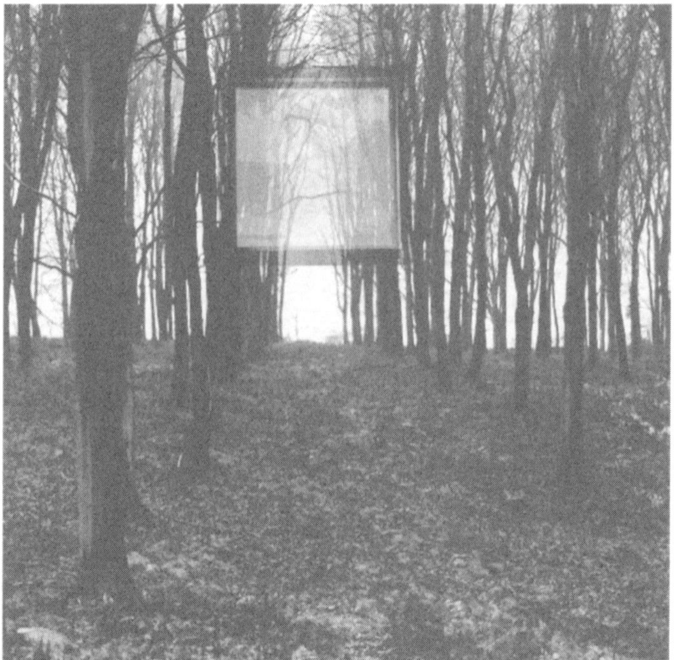

Hardwick to Chatteris

—And toward what dates do we write ourselves?
   Paul Celan, *Meridian*

The poem chooses December 5
the day of fracture
time & everything
is out of joint
boundaries
    borders
        places dissolve
into an in-between-ness & a no
where

        See Holbein's "The Ambassadors".
        Instead of viewing it straight on,
        stand very close to it on the right hand
        side. Only then does the oblong shape
        in the bottom centre reveal itself to
        be a human skull. Anamorphosis.

Today the path traces the journey in
    to landscape
not a noun but a verb
not an object to be
examined or
a text to be read but
a process marking
the trace
    of its passing

The trace defines
        withholds
                remains
after the footsteps inscribing it have passed
        drawing you backwards
                into itself

I cannot walk this way
without thinking of you

                      stand close to me now

ORDNANCE SURVEY MAP 225: HUNTINGDON & ST. IVES

Edging away from spires
    the Isle of Eels & the Ship of the Fens
        the land gives way
  to waterways & mire

no talk of fences here
    no walls
            fissures open
            clean
            rifts
            hairline cracks
            what is breathed

    won't return to much-loved land
forget its name   make action plans

Go over the A14 & right into the landing place
    of a man named Swaef
once port   once castle   once alien priory
        "steadfast in work and play"

follow Meridian to the Pathway Long Distance Walk

great crested grebes   goldeneyes doing the head-throw-kick
chiaroscuro of three black swans
        twining   land & sky

this
mushy dank day
brrrrrrrrrrrrrrrrrrrrrrrrrrrrrrrrrrrrrrrrrrrrrrrrrrrrrrrrrrrrrrrrrrrr

winter fog recalls Ghost Sark
    so far back

        Are you keeping up?

walk along the embankment to Bluntsome/Bluntesham
Webbs Hole Sluice   Swavesey Drain
    evidence of romans
        neolithic humans

here in this low-lying land
    slow canals   too shallow
        for ships

plunk of frog or toad
    a weedy ditch   water so still
        words black out
            below sea level thick with mud

Who lives here

    we   sawflies mayflies caddisflies snakeflies
            dragonflies fleas lacewings brimstone bees

    we   in water too spiny loach bitterling bream roach

    we   wild ghosts lapping

dispersed   hidden   sometimes
    underground
        suspicious

once a plethora
      we   fish astonishing
          the incomers

tithes settled by eel currency
      reeds peat rushes
          alive alive o

a lavishment of space
      & water
the youngest of landscapes
      once wooded   then flooded
they dried the land
      occupied   enclosed it
40,000 acres of fertile farmland
      how to calculate the cost
          how much is enough

I follow The Great Ouse
      straightened here   controlled there
          by sluices   [Webbs Hole Sluice
                Brownshill Lock and Staunch]

Warning: Please do not climb on any structures

      gravel extraction   constant din of diggers

INCIPIT   "man against nature" what they taught us at school
EXPLICIT   I am a woman for nature   uncontrolled

alternative facts pile up
      layer on layer
malfeasants   do nothing
      O guardian spirits

bats/bees
        apocalyptic prophecies
                God be gracious this day to bees
the doomsday clock moves
thirty seconds closer

                            ::

Somersham sits on the Meridian
        once a palace / a chase / a soke
                things got smashed   rejoined
boggy slamp   can't keep up
reorient   continue north
nothing visible   roke rising
        thick & thicker
recalculate   toold
        bonecold   herend

scucca...

Orange-tinged water
flavour of warm flat irons
Abbey founded by Bishop
Aelfren for 500 years it
henchmen destroyed it
an earthenware jar
detritus found outside town
of an elephant when
land to Ereb till ice melted

Chalybeate Springs
Hardwick to Chatteris
Aednoth & his sister
Thrived till Henry's
Three hundred years later
Early fourth century
Reportedly the skeleton
Ice age joined Engla
Sea levels rose

⬇

Fenland covered in sea
highland became island
a transition zone
Vermuyden came to
the land dried / shrank

Marshland layered in clay
At the coast the Wash
Rich in fish and fowle
Cut the land to speed the flow
Here a metre below the sea

...whose paws leave no prints

ORDNANCE SURVEY MAP 227: PETERBOROUGH

Chatteris to Guyhirn

Gone walking   miles
  of space &
    wind
train tracks & telephone lines
  spoil the land
early morning   early
  April reed warbler
    intones the Fenland sedge

  I am walking towards you

an owl startles
  escaping from ruined farmsteads
    rusted machinery [me]
recent tyre tracks
  wasted food heaps of it oranges some still edible
the seagulls
  swoop & grab

Wandering off-path
I tiptoe round the leeks
scramble up an embankment
  to the A141
  need
  to approach
  need to approach
  with care

clamber over the barrier
    down the steps
    to the track
    with Vermuyden's Drain on the right
        a landscape of nothing
        but scores of drains
        (those who financed it took it for themselves)
a field of small bridges
a ditch   a crossing
    to no where
        memory of water
    the prolonged present
    where horses pass[ed]
    cross-hatch of hooves
        stencilled in clay

once populous   charged
    with multiple varied pasts
        before the scrape
now silent   Stonea
    sits on a gravel bank
the footprint of a tower suggests
    intimidation   land of resistance
        Boudicca's last stand
    evidence of human skulls
        hacked by swords   the cleaved skull of a child

something brutal in this place
    uncanny
I take off my shoes
    to touch them
        skin to skin

At nearby Wimblington
> the darts players in the Anchor
>> stand mute
> dark silhouettes of the people they were
>> a moment ago
> silence
>> for the 7-year-old boy who died
>>> *asthma*

I slip away
> to endless fields
>> pock-marked
> by pylons   disused rail lines

pain ripples from hip to knee & back again
> trudge carefully now
> between the furrows
> hidden in long grass

>> St Wendreda's Church at March has
>> "the most splendid timber roof in
>> Cambridgeshire"
>>> (Pevsner)

120 carved angels attach to its beams
Wendreda daughter of King Anna of Angles
> healer of the sick

The Leechbook details the practice
>> bloodletting
>> horse dung to stop bleeding
>> wen salve for wounds (pepper,
>> ginger, radish, chervil, fennel, garlic, sage)

        suture with silk
        silver filings for a burn (bear grease, thyme,
        rose petals, verbena)

A pall hangs over this town
dark warnings permeate the airwaves
        threat level set to severe
meteorologists identify clouds never seen before
        asperitas / roll clouds / cirrus homogenitus
            (better known as contrails)

nitrogen dioxide exposure
causes 64 deaths a day
the government says publishing the plan
would be like dropping a controversial bomb
into the election campaign
normalizing thermonuclear war

everyone dreams of
        mushroom clouds these days
the politics of brinksmanship

rupture   the vessel
& everything inside
rolls away like marbles
on a table
what remains is
        the landscape
            of the bardo world
        between lifeanddeath

ORDNANCE SURVEY MAP 235: WISBECH & PETERBOROUGH NORTH & MAP 249: SPALDING & HOLBEACH

Guyhirn to Boston

But the season is spring
        the trail   flares
                through the furrowed field
the big eye   at the end
        doesn't blink

drainage ditches conduct field work
        overhead the cables pulse
        untranslatable messages
the buzz
        gives rise to vertigo
        soundings / static
the turbulence of a passing train
inside every crack in the earth
        is a word waiting
        to get out
stumbling in entanglements
until this moment
        I had been a walker without a path
        the miles streaming underfoot

Question: Looking back what did you learn?
Answer: Not to be afraid of emptiness

the untrodden grass is not a path
        nettles bite my legs
        leaving teeth marks
onions ripening in the fields
        later I smell them
                heaped   rotting down
        so much waste

the River Nene glides in the grip of
        the seabank
        on the north
the Chapel of Ease (1660)
        a small rectangular box
        made of brick & Barnack stone
five windows of leaded panes
        set in stone mullions
        wavy where the glass has sagged
narrow pews to prevent kneeling
        outside the gravestones
        slouch
close your eyes
        see the child
        buried in her stillbirth
her hands reach for you
        a flock of birds
        rise   fly south
my journey is the other way
north to Holbeach

::

Fertile silt
    famous for tulip bulbs & manufactured food

the trucks roll in   roll out
the earth shakes   the sky quakes
    RAF tornadoes rise from the salt marsh

on the road to Whaplode I find
an old millstone
    lie down on the Meridian
        wait for the passing

walking on   following the old Sea Bank
cocooned by thicket
where the bank has breached
    open land   big sky country
I watch the cumulonimbus approach
    carrying
        rain
    bludgeoning
        rain   high wind
    hailstone swathes
        in open land

Slippery Gowt

the sky spins
    spouts water
        pellets ice
            the old roman sea bank slumps
the stump signals
    in the distance

O Botwulf
watch over me now
for I am much afraid

isolated remnants of creeks
World War II pillboxes
    little stone rooms
        dark as a tomb
           whispering
                come on in
                it's warm and dry
                nobody here but us
                ghosts   spiders
                    bones

crows ahead
    in shiny black capes
        block the way

a brief change of weather at Frampton Marsh
    avocet
        red shank
                hen harrier
        whimbrel
    skylark

a marshy delta in coastal wilderness
    exposed
heavy weather returns
    hail & brimstone
        not done with me yet

            —then let fall
            your horrible pleasure

time is playing out   on this bank
    holding me to account
        every step opens a new rift
   of pain   the bank
a threshold   the walking of it
   a library

the trail behind vanishes
   even as I lie down on it
     I lose myself
        untangling grid lines
        my wits have turned
        time is playing out

it is true that the path must end
it will write the poem
   on the back of me

         I walked the Old Sea Bank through
         Lincolnshire
         it interrogated me
         I came out
            wanting

Write it! I say
here's the nib

Dear Paul

And toward what dates do we ~~write~~ walk? Distance and proximity. The Meridian situates itself between, acting both as a measure of distance and a marker of connectivity. Der Nullmeridian is a cartographic construct, a line that divides, a circle which binds. It relies on two opposing poles, but it exists in no place. Walking these 270 miles, I have tried to enact the process of the poem's routeness. We are both in time and of time, as we come into a space of appearance. You say, "what's real happens", breaking into the world of appearances, taking effect. Ice storms do that. One does not imagine it, one discovers it in the process of walking. In this same way, the poem needs to discover a relationship to the real in its encounter with others. As the voice who speaks the poem, I am both "I" and an altered version of "I". The poem itself is a coming to terms with loss—both actual and real, as the source of meaning. When I address you, you are not lost to me. And so I walk, and then I sleep, dreaming the poem which dreams me. It is 10:15 p.m. in Boston, Lincolnshire, and tomorrow I head toward the Humber.

Ever yours,
Nancy

Meridian: An adaptation

vocem paginarum

cleft-footed
sometimes iambic
the poem is a step
its medium is language
in conversation to say nothing
of hermeneutics
                          intentio

it starts with listening
beyond the mechanics
to the unsaid
hibernating
you are the means
by which the poem happens

with a slightly fidgety
finger on the map
you come upon your hands
searching for a place
of origin
a poemstead
I know where
such a place should be

the paths narrow
to a nettle-route
walking them
you have to keep vigil[ant]
the poem crawls ahead
a terrestrial
lizardly creature
        anguis fragilis

the trail retains something
of the historical
uncanny
very far back
in the air we breathe

the wind has gained speed
the storm surges
over the poem
testing
it stands fast   *attentio*
something immaterial
unavailable
invisible
but earthly
compass-like
returns to itself

this route
describes a circle
—I took this route
with that line
such a route
did this line take
with me

Notes to Part III

Part III is framed by the work of Paul Celan, especially his essay *The Meridian*. For Celan, poems are *en route*—they are headed toward. This brief quotation describes the criterion for every living thing as "the relatively short time span of its full appearance." The poem tries to reach across time, but never achieves this.

p.69. This acrostic poem is introduced by the word "scucca", an Old English word for evil spirit or demon.

p.76. The name of Boston's church is St. Botolph, endearingly known by locals as "The Stump," because its extraordinarily tall tower can be seen from miles around.

The quotation is from Shakespeare's *King Lear*.

p.79. This epistolary poem is based on Spicer's fictitious correspondence with Lorca in *After Lorca*. Just as *After Lorca* was a turning point for Spicer in terms of composition by book, *Meridian* marks my first attempt at writing a book-length poem. Celan's *Meridian* essay is foundational to my poetic project. In the poem that follows the letter, "vocem paginarum" appears to indicate that the poem is a cut-up of some of the key words from Celan's essay, woven together with my own, and ending on p.81 with a beautiful line by Pierre Joris, who provided the English translation of *The Meridian*. Celan suggests: "I" do not suffice without "you". Who are you? A reader, a stranger, a lover, an imaginary companion, a forest, a field, a dragonfly? You may be real. Or abstract. But by addressing you, you become visible and near, and we are part of a collective life.

IV

Boston
to Sand le Mere

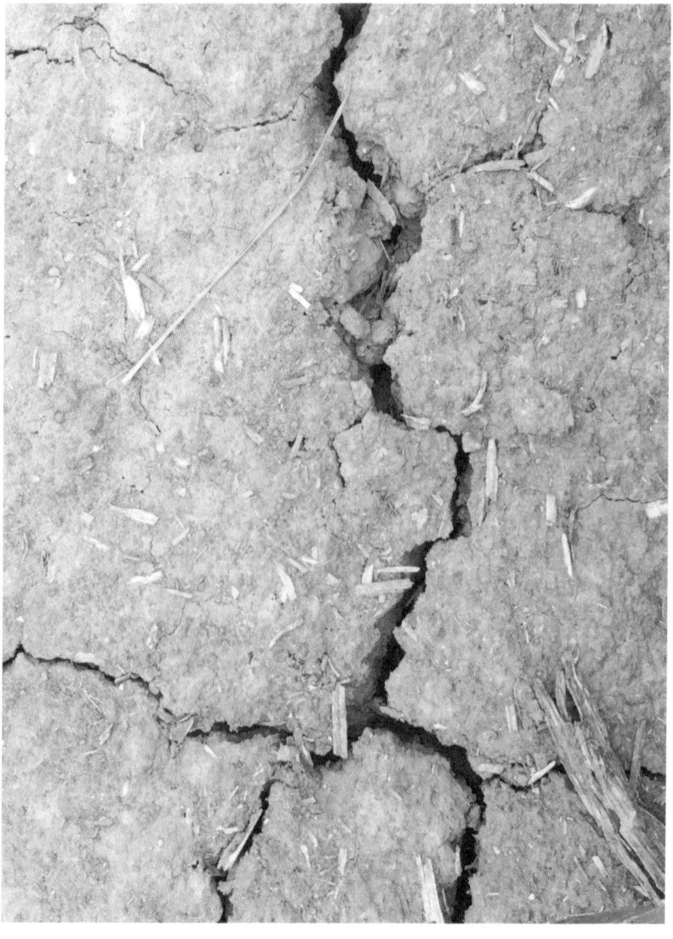

ORDNANCE SURVEY MAP 261: BOSTON

—The line, like life, has no end.
    Tim Ingold, *Lines: A Brief History*

Highest of alerts
    heaviest of hearts
        in memoriam for six dead
        scores injured on Westminster Bridge

—all bright & glittering in the smokeless air

walking again on trails born of mud
    & thought
        in memoriam for seven dead
        scores injured on London Bridge

—London Bridge will NEVER fall down

walking in a landscape of few villages
    centuries of land reclamation
        in memoriam for twenty-three dead
        250 injured in Manchester

walking past ghostly control towers
    buckled runways
        in memoriam for one dead
        ten injured at Finsbury Mosque

walking on what the map calls
    West Fen / Catchwater Drain
        in memoriam for Grenfell
        a lesion of flame searing
        the night sky

in the falling ash
  the dead whisper their names
    with swollen hands I try to catch

we are enmeshed
  with every step my heart is full
    of them

words crawl from the cracks in the clay
  they gather at my feet
    ripe for harvest

the mind unravels along medieval furrow & trough
  spiralling out through
    Lincolnshire

—*twilight & evening bell, and after that the dark*

ORDNANCE SURVEY MAP 282: LINCOLNSHIRE WOLDS NORTH

Boston to Louth

In a slow flotilla of ships, they followed John Cotton, charismatic non-conformist vicar of St Botolph, to the new world. From every hamlet, village, town

and church. At Bag Enderby the church stands on greensand, the rock that underpins the chalk hereabouts. Not the bells that Tennyson heard, but a 13th century font with a pieta that breaks

your heart. Red arrows & skylark song over Catchwater Drain. Not a military march but a slow sauntering. Walking the prime meridian wanting

methylene blue to illumine the invisible world, revealing the line I walk. When the blackbird sings I whistle, the bird replies, or so I like to think

some paths are dead ends, others lead to fords and water too deep to cross. Today the wind blows from the south. Reduced ceremonial elements. The Queen dressed in royal blue, her hat too, embellished with yellow stars. She delivers her speech. (Next year's is cancelled.) The DUP issue

low-growled threats. Temperatures top 30 for the fifth consecutive day. Another summer solstice & all the politicians change direction according to the prevailing winds. In politics the less you care, the better you do. I catch the scent of salt & fish. Nordsjön, the sea my mother & grandmother crossed a century ago, urging me closer

but every time I cross continents I am contributing to the Sixth Mass Extinction. Not absorbed for 25,000 years, the greenhouse gases from my flight. I cause it, knowing this. The catastrophe is already here. All of us are enmeshed in this.

On mother's birthday I walk the riverine / lacustrine landscape of the Lincolnshire Wolds. Tennyson's beloved Somersby is cloaked in mist. As Helen did, reciting from memory... *may there be no moaning at the bar when I put out to sea.* We are all enmeshed &

hotter still the following day. Crossing amber waves, Burwell Walk, 189 acres of arable land. Grassland host to bird's-foot trefoil, lady's bedstraw, hay rattle, bracken. Beneath them lies the shadow of ridges & troughs

the open field system of medieval farming. One furlong for each family. Enough to sustain. Now ploughed over for industrial farming... wheat, barley, sugar beets, oil seed rape... 80% lost in the last sixty years.

Pigs stunned by captive bolt pistol, the sickening thud of forceful blows. The object to destroy the cerebrum whilst keeping the heart pumping for exsanguination.

An infestation of blisters & tears slows me to a halt. Mortification of the flesh by ordnance survey map. Horse flies needing a blood meal to lay their eggs attach themselves.

    Snipes Dale. Steep chalk escarpment, old plateau grassland & a disused quarry of red chalk rich in fossils. Limestone the remains of fallen animals. Belemnites, brachiopods. Once sea animals, now meadow pipits, lizards, bee orchids, purple saxifrage. A step away

    from them. What is a ghost? A phantom crew appearing through the fog? Remembered lines, letters vibrating on paper, a double exposure, a sudden change in temperature, an animal fossilized or an insect trapped

    in amber? It was the promise of an end that led me deeper into the interior. The further I walked the more passion the line excited in me. The whole world became luminous and everywhere this luminous world was traversed by lines outlining all objects. The sun drinks me till I am nothing but white light in an empty vessel.

    Not a three-dimensional entity, but the impression of something that used to be there. Not the line

but the space between.

Louth to Fulstow

Permissive pathways
burrow through
field after field
grain swirls
indentations
where animals
slept last night

the trail bends
to over-ripe wheat
then opens
to pasture & cattle
then further still
through rosettes of broad green
leaves rich in protein
but discarded
powerless
to resist the sun
indifferent to the constancy
of the speed of light
the tuber's purple globes
curve above the soil's surface
basking in the glow
of so much light

as the farms get bigger
I grow smaller
then finally free
in the space surrounding me
I am nothing

but a tiny speck of blue
in a yellow cornfield
blue the colour of longing
the sea at the edge
of the horizon
the back range of the mountains
the clouds resembling them

When people came
from the old world
to the new
they brought their seeds
plants, animals, names
failing to embrace
where they were
but gradually learning
the language of the place

gussock, moor-gallop, piner, windin'

I press the line
a creation of geography & mathematics
marked out for merchants
& military ships
into the Wolds
extending beyond flatness
into a confluence
of surface & space
present & past
the walk an articulation
of ground   I compel
the line to speak
in real time

bringing memories
from past into present
seeing clearly now what
Larkin saw—*where sky*
and Lincolnshire and water meet

The mind wanders
with voluptuous sadness
the landscapes of memory
& desire
like fragile skin
so easily torn
by a thorn
terra incognita
the maps once called it
but no map reveals
all that there is
I sleep with
my head pointed North
as Clare did
towards the imperishable stars

At the end of the day
I come back indoors to
news of Charlottesville
an act of domestic terrorism
white men with torches
chanting blood & soil
POTUS says they're
"all good people"
I cannot will not fall
into line

In the middle
of an August day
all over America
the sky grows dark
I watch you sleeping
your mouth open
in the shape of a scream
and I think I don't want
to live in this world
anymore   something
has shifted
this is just
the beginning

ORDNANCE SURVEY MAP 283:
LOUTH & MABLETHORPE

Fulstow to Cleethorpes

Today I walk out
of my own knowledge
& into quag
stepping firmly without
letting the foot sink too low
maintaining forward thrust
against the slop
holding the heel down to hear
the suck & pop
as the sump gives way

my life a map
traced on this terrain
I write with my feet
tramping the path
into recognition
ahead a woman
in a floral dress
disappears into a wall
of leaves
when I reach the
place she was
a ghostly electricity
raises the hairs on my arms

I follow the beast trails
footprint of badger, red fox, roe deer
those who were here
before   a continuous flow

Saharan desert-dwelling ants
count their own steps
enabling them to use
dead-reckoning
like them we are edge-
dwellers in an ever-shifting
landscape
the living & the dead
the dreamers
the animals
the water babies
      the wind

Speaking place-names

    Fulstow, Tetney, Humberston, Cleethorpes

I walk that way
the names lure me
across the landscape
binding sole to earth
      smoothness of mind
      resilience of mind
      steadiness of mind

a Midwestern prairie nomad
born in the middle of the last century
with a portable past

      place is where things happened

On the lee of the canal
I mistake a swan nesting
for a white stone
she raises her enormous wings
tucks in her neck
to warn me off

I walk into the blank space
on the map
while overhead
the wind turbines
blade the air
in a futile attempt
to halt climate change

Deep & deeper
into my lungs
I breathe in this space
marshland reclaimed
from the sea by the hands
of individuals
I breathe in
the early settlements
of mud huts on the dykes
& willow-lined ditches & later
scattered farmsteads
on the chalk & limestone uplands
& later villages lost
to the plague & enclosure
the only visible sign
of their existence
a foundation

of rubble   shallow
depressions marking former
thoroughfares
unrewarding chalk soil
knuckles of flint
some geologists take
to be petrified sponge

I pass a single isolated
farmstead of slate & stone
squatting under a clump
of sycamores
walking the old drove roads
where hardly ever a human
voice is heard
in the absence of the living
I walk with ghosts

Each night we sleep in our own time zone
with another 1.8 billion people
as the sea levels rise &
the Arctic sea ice melts
faster than even the scientists predicted
people are booking
cruises to see it
Mars is uninhabitable
but nations are racing to colonise it

At Cleethorpes I delay
climbing up to the sea bank
two years & forty days
after I started it

my companion pulls me up anyway
running until he's
knee-deep in swirling water
mesmerised
his tail a propeller
of great round arcs
I share his joy for a moment
letting go of all that is happening

    not in my name

I have walked from Peacehaven
to the mouth of the Humber
some 200 miles
taking this distance as the length
of the history of the universe
13.7 billion years
human life on this planet
is less than a single step

But the Meridian doesn't end here
across the Humber into the East Riding
I go   but first
a detour to the west
& the Humber Bridge

Barton-upon-Humber → Hessle

suspended
in air
on
Humber Bridge
an umbilical
cord
connecting
Lincolnshire
to
Yorkshire

::

upriver
the Trent
& Ouse
converge

::

mudflats
saltmarsh
reed beds
samphire

::

fresh water
flows
out
to sea
draining
one-fifth
of the country

::

sandbanks
& islands
lie along
shoreline
brackish
lagoons
a vast
expanse
teeming
with
invertebrates
worms
molluscs
::
avocets
oystercatchers
curlew
scurry
with
the ebb
& flow
picking
at water
heavy
with
sediment
::
this
coast
is
sinking
each
winter

the sea
takes
more
the movement
of the waves
counterintuitive
don't
look
down
O
::
the wind
plays
the cables
the towers
wider
at the top
vibrate
with the passing
of traffic
the pitch
carries
over
the sea
to
the North
pole
the bridge
bends
to
the earth's
curve

O
will
it
ever
end
::
at
the mouth
of the estuary
the silver
sickle
of
Spurn Head
Raven's
Promontory
like
Aphrodite
born
of tide &
shifting sand
then lost
to the sea
that
took
it all
even the dead
in
their graves

ORDNANCE SURVEY MAP 292: WITHERNSEA & SPURN HEAD

Patrington to Sand le Mere

Over thousands of years
longshore drift
Spurn Head
shifts west
I follow the trail
on this side
of the estuary

through unremarkable flats
& bungalows
at Patrington
a pair of whalebones
set into small brick plinths
recalls an earlier time
I walk towards Withernsea
through Hollym
stopping at
The Plough Inn
the only customer
in one of few buildings left
made of wattle & daub

the land soggy
low-lying wetlands
overgrown
with many
drains
diversions

the path
sometimes
a channel
I wade through
skin changes to scale
I keep an eye
on the seabank
a blue heron ascends
skimming its legs
on the water's
surface

with talon-hands
I pull myself up
the sea bank
tugging
at long tufts of grass
a wind and water creature
there it is
ripple patches
at low tide
but further out
a current of turquoise
shining in late afternoon
sunlight

that is where I want to be
shedding
this human skin
to join the seals out there
where the Meridian line
takes leave of the land
surging further
and further
north

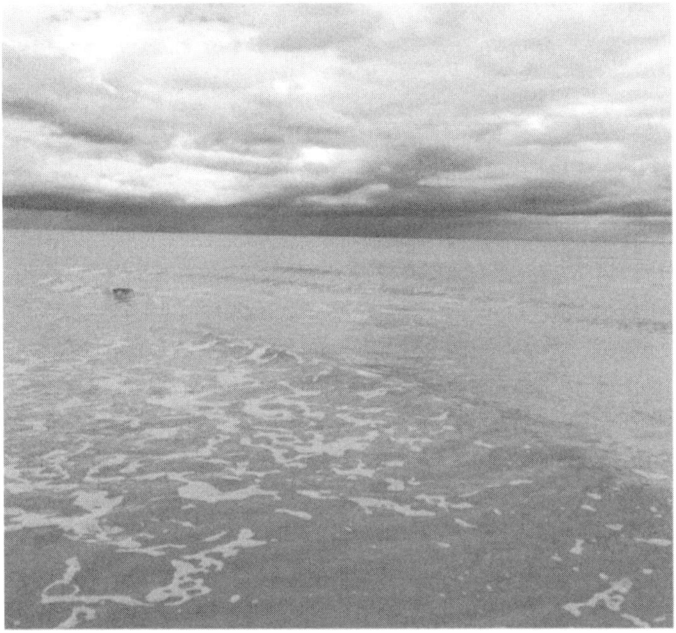

Notes to Part IV

Part IV begins with an epigraph from Tim Ingold's *Lines: A Brief History*. Throughout this project the notion of lines has preoccupied me, and I have found many useful guides, such as Ingold, but also Rebecca Solnit's *A Field Guide to Getting Lost*, and Chet Raymo's *Walking Zero*. But it seems most appropriate to end the project with a reminder that the Meridian is actually a circle that never ends.

p.85. The line "all bright and glittering in the smokeless air" is from Wordsworth's poem 'Composed upon Westminster Bridge September 3, 1802'.

The line "London Bridge will NEVER fall down" was scrawled onto an *Evening Standard* banner.

p.86. As I was walking through Tennyson's Somersby, these events were occurring—thus, the final line from 'Crossing the Bar'.

p.88. Amongst the Helen Adam papers and archives at the Poetry Collection, University Libraries, University at Buffalo, is a photograph of Helen's sister, Pat, with Tennyson's poem 'Crossing the Bar' written in Helen's hand.

p.91. The words "gussock", "moor-gallop", "piner" and "windin'" come from Robert Macfarlane's *Landmarks*.

p.92. You can't walk through Lincolnshire without recalling Larkin's 'The Whitsun Weddings'.

p.98. This calculation of the distance is from Chet Raymo's *Walking Zero*.

pp.99-102. The Humber Bridge is off-route; the Meridian Line crosses the Humber estuary. You can travel it by boat, or, as in this case, go further inland and cross the Humber Bridge.

Bibliography

Adam, Helen. *Turn Again To Me and Other Poems*. New York: Kulchur Foundation, 1977.

Blake, William. *Songs of Innocence and of Experience*. www.bl.uk/collection-items/william-blakes-songs-of-innocence-and-experience

Celan, Paul. *The Meridian*. Trans. Pierre Joris. Stanford: Stanford University Press, 2011.

Clare, John. *The Complete Works of John Clare*. Delphi Classics, 2013.

Dickens, Charles. *Our Mutual Friend*. Ware, Herts: Wordsworth Classics, 1997.

Flanagan, Richard. *The Narrow Road to the Deep North*. London: Chatto & Windus, 2014.

Gizzi, Peter. *The House That Jack Built: The Collected Lectures of Jack Spicer*. Middletown, CT: Wesleyan, 1998.

Ingold, Tim. *Lines: A Brief History*. London: Routledge, 2016.

Macfarlane, Robert. *Landmarks*. London: Hamish Hamilton, 2015.

Moor, Robert. *On Trails: An Exploration*. London: Aurum, 2016.

Niedecker, Lorine. *Collected Works*. Berkeley, CA: University of California Press, 2002.

Olson, Charles. *The Maximus Poems*. Berkeley, CA: University of California Press, 1992.

—*Collected Prose*. Berkeley, CA: University of California Press, 1997.

Pasternak, Boris. *My Sister—Life*. Trans. Mark Rudman. Evanston, IL: Northwestern University Press, 1983.

Raymo, Chet. *Walking Zero*. New York: Walker & Company, 2006.

Sinclair, Iain. *Lights Out for the Territory*. London: Penguin, 2003.

—. *Edge of the Orison: In the Traces of John Clare's 'Journey Out of Essex'*. London, Penguin, 2005.

Solnit, Rebecca. *A Field Guide to Getting Lost*. Edinburgh: Canongate, 2005.

Spicer, Jack. *After Lorca*. London: Aloes Books, 1969.

Twain, Mark. *Life on the Mississippi*. Ware, Herts: Wordsworth, 2012.

Whitman, Walt. *The Complete Poems*. London: Penguin, 1996.

Acknowledgements

Many people have helped during the planning and walking of the Greenwich Meridian Trail. Initial and heart-felt thanks to Graham and Hilda Heap, whose four guidebooks, *Greenwich Meridian Trail*, were a constant source of guidance and inspiration. As luck would have it, I ran into them on the trail outside Waltham Abbey. They were posting way-markers on a footbridge I was crossing, and I overheard Hilda say, "She's carrying the book." They were smiling broadly when I met them and they introduced themselves to me. We walked a couple of miles together that day.

Thanks to people who gave me accommodation en route. This includes Nicola Schmidt-Renfree, with whom I stayed on the first night's walk from Peacehaven to Lewes. Patricia Debney offered me hospitality through the Fens and kept track of me whilst I walked the most difficult sections through Lincolnshire.

Thanks to Peter Hughes, who published an earlier version of Part I of *Meridian* through Oystercatcher in spring of 2016. I am extremely grateful to Peter Riley, who wrote so generously of my work, including a burb for the pamphlet, *Meridian* (Part I). And to Brian Lewis (Longbarrow Press) for his review of my work to date, and especially for its publication. I am also grateful to Linda Black and Lucy Hamilton, who published the first few pages of Part II (Greenwich to Hardwick) in *Long Poem Magazine*, and Iain Sinclair, who spoke to me about an early draft of *Meridian* whilst he was a visiting professor at Kent. Special thanks to the Poetry Collection at the University of Buffalo (Edric Mesmer, Alison Fraser and James Maynard) for their invitation to read a section of *Meridian* in October 2016 whilst I was researching in the Helen Adam archives. Thanks also to Scarlett Thomas and her invitation for me to present *Meridian* as a work in progress at the University of Kent. I am also grateful to Louis Rowan who invited me to publish a section of this work in his magazine, *The Golden Handcuffs Review*.

I am grateful for those who accompanied me on the walk, either in person (Katherine Peddie) or in spirit (Helen Adam, John Clare, Paul Celan).

Thanks too to my two stepsons John and Richard Vile, who encouraged me with books and science. I might have given up without the help of John and Sarah at the point where it looked like I might have to abandon it.

So many people cheered me along the way, or helped with directions when they were needed. Notable was Albi Cozens who collected me from remote places in Lincolnshire to take me to my accommodation, too many miles away to walk to in a single day, and the nameless people I met on the walk who were a constant source of delight.

THANK YOU to my husband who provided constant love and encouragement throughout this, to my daughter, Erin Hartley Price, who is the reason, to my grandchildren, Aspen and Taylor Price, whose love keeps me keeping on, to my brother and sister, John and Wendy Gaffield, who share this story. Special thanks to Dana Starr, who led me to "Meridian", and big love to poets David Herd and Patricia Debney, mentors and friends.